THE
TRUTH
ABOUT
HELL

John Blanchard

EP Books (Evangelical Press), 1st Floor Venture House, 6 Silver Court, Watchmead, Welwyn Garden City, UK, AL7 1TS

admin@epbooks.org

www.epbooks.org

In the USA EP Books are distributed by:
JPL Books, 3883 Linden Ave. S.E., Wyoming, MI 49548

order@jplbooks.com

www.jplbooks.com

ISBN 978-1-78397-208-1

INTRODUCTION

'Hell' is a very popular word, though it is used to mean many different things. To go 'hell for leather' is to go as fast as possible; to have 'a snowball's chance in hell' is to have no chance at all; to 'raise hell' is to cause trouble; to be 'as angry as hell' is to be furious; 'hell's bells' is used to express anger or surprise; to give a person 'merry hell' is to give them a hard time; to 'try like hell' is to try one's best.

'Hell' can define something as being difficult or dangerous. When my stepmother faced critical surgery, the surgeon told me that she was facing 'a hell of an operation.' On the other hand, it can mean something very enjoyable. When England's cricketers finally won a game on a demoralizing tour of matches in Australia, their captain told the press, 'Winning beats the hell out of losing.' It can also mean using a great deal of power or effort. In his book *How to play your best golf all the time*, the famous Scottish golfer Tommy Armour advised his readers to 'whack the hell out of the ball with the right hand' (though I am sure he meant the opposite for left-handers!). There are even many times when 'Hell!' alone is enough to express anger, frustration or disappointment.

'Hell' may be a very popular word, but hell is a hugely unpopular subject, one that people try to avoid thinking about and have no enthusiasm for exploring. Yet because the subject is massively important these pages are written to help you do both.

One of the reasons (but not the main one) why many people shy away from thinking or talking about hell is that it is a religious subject, and religion turns them off. Yet it is impossible to get even the faintest idea of what hell means without accepting that it has a religious context; virtually every major religion in the world teaches something that at least relates to the general idea of what hell is about.

The word 'hell' can be traced back to a Germanic origin: it came into Old English as *hel* (a spelling it still retains in Dutch) probably with the Saxons. Digging back even further, the trail eventually leads to two of the oldest languages in the world still in common use— Hebrew and Greek—and to get a clear understanding of what hell means we need to find a reliable source where words meaning hell are widely used. There is only one such source, the Bible, in which words we now translate 'hell' occur about 150 times. If we are serious about discovering what hell really means we need to get a clear picture of what the Bible says about it.

This immediately raises a problem for those who, even without reading it, think the Bible is a collection of religious myths and fables cobbled together thousands of years ago, so write it off as having no authority and no relevance to them in today's world. Yet as it is the database for everything that follows in this booklet, we need to check whether this is the case, or whether we can trust it to be telling us the truth. *If you have questions about the authority and integrity of the Bible, you may want to read the Appendix (*Why you can trust the Bible*) to this booklet before going any further.*

By every test that we can apply, the Bible proves to be true and trustworthy. Everything it says is true, but it does not tell us everything. For example, it tells us nothing about the depth of the Atlantic Ocean, the law of gravity, or the mating habits of turtles. Its core message is about God and humanity and their relationship to each other, and everything it says fits into that central message. Because hell is one of its key subjects, we can be confident that the Bible tells us the truth about it.

HELL IS FACTUAL

On the roof of Liverpool's John Lennon Airport are painted the words, 'Above us, only sky.' The words are from the John Lennon song *Imagine,* ranked by one UK survey as the second-best single of all time. Yet when we read the whole of the song's first verse, the message says much more:

> Imagine there's no heaven.
> It's easy if you try;
> No hell below us,
> Above us only sky,
> Imagine all the people living for today.

Nobody can be sure why Lennon wrote these words, or what he meant by them, though as we find elsewhere in the song, he is dreaming of a world with 'no countries', 'no religion' and 'no possessions' (interesting, as he was a millionaire at the time). The two phrases about his make-believe world that need to get our attention at this point are 'no heaven' and 'no hell below us,' because this famous song is related to a question millions of people have been asking for thousands of years: *what happens when we die?*

Lennon asks us to imagine that death is the end of the human story, and that when we die we cease to exist. This idea—called annihilationism—has been around for thousands of years. In ancient times the Greek philosopher Epicurus said, 'When death is present we no longer exist,' and in modern times a Director of the British Humanist Association claims, 'Life leads to nothing.' At first glance, this seems like an attractive idea. It means that we will never be held accountable for any of the wrong things in our lives, so we might as well do our own thing, live any way we like, and hang the consequences. Any pride, selfishness, immorality, dishonesty and other negative behaviour will simply die with us. Even whether we believed in God, let alone tried to obey him, will be irrelevant.

Yet before we sign up to this, we need to realize that it means there will never be any final justice. Serial killers and children who die in infancy, murderous terrorists and gentle, law-abiding citizens, paedophiles and peace-makers will all have the same destiny and be wiped out of existence the moment they die. Something jars here. Speaking after the 9/11 terrorist attack on the United States in 2001, US President George Bush said of those who planned it, 'Either they will be brought to justice, or justice will be brought to them.' He probably meant justice in this life, reflecting our instinct that justice should be done and be seen to be done. Yet he may also have hinted at something more—the Bible's teaching that not only is it 'appointed for man to die once' but that 'after that comes judgement,'[1] when we will come

---

[1]   Hebrews 9:27

face to face with God, 'the Judge of all the earth'[2] and give an account of our lives.

As we do, we will be faced with two seriously challenging facts. The first is God's complete and perfect knowledge of everything we have ever thought, said or done. It is suggested that every person living in Great Britain is captured on a CCTV camera an average of 300 times a day, more often than in any other country. Yet these cameras record only a small fraction of what we do, and nothing of what we think or say. On the other hand, God is 'perfect in knowledge'[3] and every detail of our lives will be 'exposed to the eyes of him to whom we must give account.'[4] Nobody who treats this trivially is thinking seriously.

The second is God's righteous anger. To many people, the idea that God can be angry seems strange or downright wrong. Whenever they think about God, they imagine him as a God of love, mercy, kindness and forgiveness. He is certainly all of these, but if we stop there all we have is a God we have invented. The Bible speaks more about God's holiness and his anger at ungodliness than it does about any of his other attributes. His name is called his 'holy name' more often than all other biblical descriptions of him. In his perfect holiness, God is utterly intolerant of sin, and 'cannot look at wrong.'[5] This does not mean that he never sees

---

[2] Genesis 18:25

[3] Job 37:16

[4] Hebrews 4:13

[5] Habakkuk 1:13

it (we have already made that point) but that he cannot ignore or overlook it. The Bible specifically says of God's home in heaven that 'nothing unclean will ever enter it.'[6] As someone has said, 'If God is holy at all, if God has an ounce of justice in his character... how could he possibly be anything else but angry with us?... A God of love who has no wrath is no God.' Yet God's anger at sin is not out of control or 'over the top'; it is an expression of his perfect holiness and justice.

It is dangerous to ignore these two facts, because they eliminate the whole idea that when we die we are annihilated, so have nothing to face or fear. The truth is exactly the opposite. Nothing in the Bible is clearer than this: there will be a final and universal day of judgement. God has 'fixed a day on which he will judge the world.'[7] With all of the future at his disposal, he has singled out a day when every human being's account will be settled once and for all. That day is firmly fixed in God's schedule and its certainty should be just as firmly settled in our minds.

THE VERDICTS

Not only is the Bible clear that we will all stand before God on the final day of judgement, it also makes it clear that everyone will be judged 'for what he has done in the body'[8]—that is to say, while living here on earth. In

---

6   Revelation 21:27

7   Acts 17:31

8   2 Corinthians 5:10

the fifteenth century the Roman Catholic Church made the complicated doctrine of purgatory its official teaching, purgatory being the place to which human souls were said to go immediately after death to be punished and purified until they were fit to go into God's presence. This process could take between a few hours and thousands of years, depending on how much purging was needed. However, the time could be shortened by the prayers and gifts of friends still living on earth, by priests saying masses on their behalf, or by visiting and venerating items decreed by the church to be holy relics. This soon led to the church selling indulgences (the reduction of time in purgatory), which became so widespread that it has been called 'the goldmine of the priesthood.' The completion of St Peter's Cathedral in Rome was financed to a large extent by indulgences granted by Pope Leo X. Indulgences are no longer blatantly hawked around, but the doctrine of purgatory remains a part of Roman Catholic teaching today, even though there is not a single statement in the Bible to back it up. Incidentally, this means that prayers for the dead are pointless. The Bible tells us that our spiritual state is sealed the moment we die, and this is how we will stand before God in judgement. The Bible likens a person's death to a tree uprooted by a storm, and says that 'where the tree falls, there it will lie.'[9] This tells us that nobody's character changes between death and judgement day. Our destinies are settled at death, after which there will be no opportunity to rectify our mistakes, overcome our weaknesses, or improve in any

---

[9]   Ecclesiastes 11:3

way. We will then be no more able to influence our destiny than a runner who has finished a race can influence the result by continuing to run.

On the final day of judgement we will not be on trial. In a trial, the judge has to hear the evidence before he pronounces a verdict, but on judgement day no evidence will be given, as none will be needed—God knows everything. Instead, he will announce the verdicts and sentences he has already determined. There will be no witnesses called, no exhibits produced, and no jury. The final day of judgement will not be an investigation, but a revelation: 'God's righteous judgement will be revealed.'[10] There will be a public unveiling of his verdicts, after which everyone who has ever lived will go to one of two eternal destinies—heaven or hell. I have written extensively elsewhere about heaven (*The Hitchhiker's Guide to Heaven* and *Anyone for Heaven,* both published by EP Books) so we can concentrate here on the subject of this booklet.

There are three original words translated 'hell' in our English versions of the Bible. The first is the Hebrew word *Sheol.* This is used to mean different but related things, such as death and the grave, but there are also places where it means a place of punishment for the wicked. For example, we are told, 'The wicked shall return to Sheol, all the nations that forget God.'[11] The second word is the Greek *Hades.* As with *Sheol,* it is used to mean more than one thing, including people being

---

[10]   Romans 2:5

[11]   Psalm 9:17

14

'brought down to Hades,'[12] a place of punishment for the ungodly. The third word is the Greek *Gehenna*, which occurs twelve times in the New Testament, including a warning that hypocritical evildoers will be 'sentenced to hell.'[13]

These three words all make it clear that hell is not fiction, but a fact. Some people try to slide around this by saying that as the entire Bible points to his authority it would be safer to rely on what Jesus said, rather than pick out statements elsewhere in the Bible, but doing this makes the reality of hell even clearer, as eleven of the twelve times *Gehenna* is used in the New Testament, Jesus is the speaker. He spoke more about the day of judgement and hell than about anything else, and referred to them in more than half of his forty parables. Some say they pin their faith on what Jesus said in the well-known Sermon on the Mount, yet in that sermon Jesus referred to hell several times, and warned of the danger of being 'thrown into hell.'[14] It is impossible to read what the Bible says and the warnings Jesus gave, and at the same time ignore or deny the reality and the certainty of hell.

---

[12]   Matthew 11:23

[13]   Matthew 23:33

[14]   Matthew 5:29

HELL IS FEARFUL

Virtually every religion teaches some form of punishment after death for wrong done here on earth. One strand of Islamic doctrine says that the wicked will endure seven grades of punishment, including being roasted and boiled. Another says they will be burned until their skins are destroyed, at which point they will be given new skins so that the punishment can be repeated. Classical Buddhism has seven 'hot hells' surrounded by torture chambers that include fiery pits and quagmires. Hinduism has twenty-one hells, tailor-made to match each person's earthly behaviour. Jainism, a spin-off from Hinduism, has no fewer than 8,400,000 hells, as well as a bottomless abyss where the worst offenders are kept for ever. These ideas are all human inventions, and can be safely ignored, but they do reflect many people's instinct that after death human beings will be accountable for how they spent their lives here on earth, and that evil will be punished.

Over the centuries, poets and other authors have expressed their visions of hell in lurid detail. The most famous of these was the Italian poet Dante Alighieri (usually known as Dante), who in his most famous work pictured hell as a vast pit shaped like an inverted cone, with its lowest point at the centre of the earth. Nine circles, each filled with thousands of people being tortured by monsters and devils, lead down to its lowest point, a frozen lake where the devil is in direct control of the punishment. In the poem, Dante tells of people shrieking and moaning, and tearing each other with their teeth, while over the gate of hell are the words, 'Abandon all hope ye who enter here.' In the eighteenth century, the English poet John Milton wrote *Paradise Lost*, in which he pictured hell as a place of 'hideous ruin and combustion' ending in 'bottomless perdition' where the victims lay 'vanquished, rolling in the fiery gulf.'

Far from being frightened by pictures like these, some people use them to mock the whole idea of hell. One humanist told BBC Radio, 'I have no fear of being confined to an eternal shish kebab.' Then what are we to make of these ideas, and of other descriptions of hell that have monsters and reptiles, boiling mud, red-hot ovens, people hanging by their hair, and others with blood gushing out of every pore? The answer is that we can safely put them out of our minds, as there is not a word in the Bible to back them up. Those who invented them took the general idea of evil being punished after death, then let their imaginations run riot. But human imagination is no substitute for divine revelation. Only God can tell us the truth about hell, and he has done so in the Bible. Although we find no gruesomely extravagant pictures there, we do discover that hell is truly fearful. Of the images the Bible gives, a few will be enough to make that clear.

Firstly, *it is pictured as a rubbish dump*. The Valley of Hinnom, just south-east of Jerusalem, was notorious in Jewish history as the place where pagan kings offered human sacrifices, even their own sons. Later, it became a public rubbish dump, in which offal and filth were poured. Later still, the bodies of dead animals and the corpses of executed criminals were flung there and left to rot. Worms bred and fed in the filth, and smoke from the fires that were always burning there added to the stench. The Jewish name for this place was *Ge Hinnom*, and this is the root of *Gehenna*, the word Jesus used eleven times when speaking about hell, including the warning he gave in the Sermon on the Mount to those whose behaviour made them liable to 'the hell of fire.'[15]

I find visiting the local council rubbish dump a strange experience. Everything I see there is an item thrown away by its owner as no longer being of any value. There is paper, metal, wood, pottery and glass, refuse from people's gardens and rubbish from their homes, everything from chromium to cardboard, plastic to polystyrene—and all of it thrown away. The dump is a wasteland. Even when full it has a feeling of emptiness. Whenever I am there, I never take a deep breath, or stop to admire the scenery. Instead, I unload and leave, glad to turn my back on it all.

---

[15]   Matthew 5:22

That dump often makes me think of hell—and the link is not far-fetched. Speaking of those whose religion was a formal pretence, Jesus compared them to salt which had lost its saltiness, then added, 'It is of no use either for the soil or for the manure pile. It is thrown away.'[16] However much we wince at the thought, hell is God's cosmic rubbish dump, and all who go there become the garbage of the universe—wasted and worthless. As C. S. Lewis puts it, 'To enter hell is to be banished from humanity. What is cast (or casts itself) into hell is not a man; it is 'remains.''

Secondly, *hell is pictured as a prison.* One of the clearest pictures Jesus gave was in one of his parables, which were simple stories to illustrate a moral or spiritual lesson. The story was about a king's servant who was sent to prison for cruel behaviour, and Jesus warned his hearers that God would do the same to them if they behaved in that way. Elsewhere, when urging people to get right with God while they had the opportunity to do so, he likened this to settling a lawsuit out of court to avoid the possibility of imprisonment.

When I was a teenager on the Channel Island of Guernsey, I lived only a few hundred yards from the island's prison, and my emotions were stirred whenever I walked past it. When I became Secretary to the States of Guernsey Prison Board, I went into the prison regularly in the course of my duties, and my emotions were even stronger when I saw men and women whose behaviour had led them to be locked away from society.

---

16   Luke 14:35

Earthly prisons vary in their conditions and amenities, from the primitive, and in some countries even barbaric, to those with more creature comforts than their inmates would normally enjoy outside. Some criminals have even been known to reoffend in order to get back inside. As we pull together the Bible's profile of hell, we will see that the contrast between earthly prisons and the eternal prison of hell could not be greater. In hell there will be no comforts or pleasures, nor will there be any facilities for pleasant rest or recreation. Hell will make the worst earthly prison seem like a holiday camp.

There is another radical difference. Earthly prisons confine only the body; the spirit can still be free—to worship, create, imagine, anticipate and hope. Earthly prisoners may also have opportunities to work, study, pass examinations, learn a trade, and gain some dignity for themselves. In the seventeenth century the English writer John Bunyan was often imprisoned for preaching the Bible's message, but while he was incarcerated he wrote *Pilgrim's Progress,* one of the best-known Christian books ever written. In a United Kingdom local council election in 1992, one candidate conducted his campaign from a prison cell in Glasgow, and won a seat on Glasgow District Council. Things are very different in hell where both 'soul and body'[17] are crippled and confined with no hope of anything ever changing for the better. In the prison of hell, there is neither the instinct nor the opportunity to achieve anything. The inmates are

---

[17]   Matthew 10:28

helpless, hopeless and powerless, and utterly drained of all ideas and inspiration.

Thirdly, *hell is pictured as a pit.* An Old Testament writer says of an evil person, 'He makes a pit, digging it out, and falls into the hole that he has made.'[18] We dare not miss the point being made here. It says that the whole life of a godless person is a process of scooping out the pit into which they will eventually fall when they die, which means that the more sin a person commits, the deeper the pit becomes. As C. S. Lewis puts it, 'The doors of hell are locked on the inside.' Nor can the wicked prevent this happening, as 'God will cast them down into the pit of destruction.'[19]

Fourthly, *hell is pictured as a place of darkness.* One of the fullest expressions of this is in the Old Testament, which describes it as 'the land of darkness and deep shadow, the land of gloom like thick darkness, like deep shadow without any order, where light is as thick darkness.'[20] Centuries later, Jesus warned those who rejected him that they would be 'thrown into the outer darkness.'[21] In the parable from which we quoted earlier, the king's attendants were told to take the cruel servant and 'cast him into the outer darkness.'[22] In another parable a slave owner told his staff to take a

---

18   Psalm 7:15

19   Psalm 55:23

20   Job 10:21-22

21   Matthew 8:12

22   Matthew 22:13

servant who had mishandled funds entrusted to him and 'cast the worthless servant into the outer darkness.'[23]

Elsewhere in the New Testament the writers get straight to the point. One writes of those who 'indulge in the lust of defiling passion and despise authority', who have 'eyes full of adultery,' are 'insatiable for sin' and 'have hearts trained in greed' then says that 'for them the gloom of utter darkness has been reserved.'[24] Another New Testament writer uses a similar expression in condemning those with grossly sinful lifestyles, 'for whom the gloom of utter darkness has been reserved for ever.'[25]

The Bible gives no explanation of what this 'darkness' means, but as 'God is light'[26] and darkness is the opposite of light, the description could not possibly be more negative. It is also worth noting that Jesus did not describe hell as 'darkness' but as '*the* darkness,' as if to emphasize that it will be infinitely worse than any physical, moral, mental or spiritual darkness ever experienced here on earth. It is virtually impossible for us to imagine a place with no delightful dawns, no gradually brightening mornings, not a single ray of sunshine, no clear sky, and none of the glorious colours we sometimes see at sunset. Nor can we find words to describe a place where 'light is as thick as darkness,' yet all of these things are true of hell.

---

[23]   Matthew 25:30

[24]   2 Peter 2:10,14,17

[25]   Jude 13

[26]   1 John 1:5

THE PAINS OF HELL

A theologian has said that it is unwise to claim 'any knowledge of either the furniture of heaven or of the temperature of hell.' This was his way of saying that when we keep to the teaching of the Bible there are limits to what we know. As far as hell is concerned, we have just seen that the Bible points us to some of its features (a rubbish dump, a prison, a pit, and darkness), but in contrast to the gruesome, blood-curdling descriptions invented by poets and others, the Bible is very restrained when speaking about the *experience* of those who will be there, and two of its statements will be sufficient here.

The first is Jesus saying of those in hell, 'their worm does not die.'[27] Jesus was quoting from an Old Testament prophet, who says of the bodies of God's enemies, 'their worm shall not die... and they shall be an abhorrence to all flesh.'[28] To liken being in hell to the picture of maggots eating rotting corpses is horrific, but what does the Bible mean?

The first thing to notice is that Jesus did not speak of '*the* worm' but of '*their* worm,' as if to emphasize that this was something internal rather than external, something personal, not general, and as their worm never dies, the reference seems to be to their conscience. A guilty conscience can be agonizingly painful. King Charles IX of France, whose reign during the mid-

---

[27]   Mark 9:48

[28]   Isaiah 66:24

sixteenth century was marred by his fierce persecution of Christians, is reported to have told his doctor, 'For months I have been in a fever physically and spiritually. If only I had spared the innocent, the weak-minded and crippled, I might get some sleep. But my conscience torments me day and night.'

Yet however severe the pangs of conscience on earth, they are infinitely greater in hell, where the wicked will endure suffering far beyond any they had on earth, and where their consciences will be their worst tormentors. There are times when we can smother our consciences, or at least tone them down, but in hell there will be no way in which they can be stifled or silenced. Conscience will make people constantly and agonizingly aware that they deliberately chose the lifestyle that condemned them. It will force them to admit the truth of every charge God brings against them, and the justice of every pain they suffer. As if this were not horrifying enough, the suffering will be uninterrupted; those enduring it will have 'no rest, day or night.'[29] As never before, they will discover the truth that, 'There is no peace ... for the wicked.'[30]

The second thing the Bible teaches about the suffering endured in hell is that 'there will be weeping and gnashing of teeth.'[31] Jesus used the phrase more than any other when warning us of the pains of hell. What does 'weeping and gnashing of teeth' mean?

---

[29]   Revelation 14:11

[30]   Isaiah 48:22

[31]   Matthew 8:12

25

'Weeping' is a very strong word, indicating much more than tears (which can also be associated with joy and laughter). 'Weeping' means tears of terrible grief, and the weeping of the wicked in hell will be triggered by all the factors which make hell so terrible—the environment, the company, the remorse, the torment and agony, the shame and contempt and the never-ending sense of God's anger.

The phrase 'gnashing of teeth' focuses on another emotion. At one point in his life, when a man called Job felt at the end of his tether, he cried out, '[God] has torn me in his wrath and hated me; he has gnashed his teeth at me.'[32] When Stephen (the first Christian martyr) was about to be stoned to death he accused his persecutors of betraying and murdering Jesus, the Son of God. As a result 'they were enraged, and they ground their teeth at him.'[33] These two examples tell us that the gnashing or grinding of teeth is a way of expressing anger. In hell, that anger will be more intense than any this world has ever experienced. The wicked will be angry at the things which gave them pleasure on earth but now give them pain in hell; angry at the sins that wrecked their lives; angry at themselves for being who they are; angry at the temptations which led them into sin and even angry at God for condemning them to their dreadful fate.

No weeping on earth can compare to the weeping in hell and no anger on earth can compare to the anger in

---

[32]   Job 16:9

[33]   Acts 7:54

hell. In the original Greek, the Bible does not speak of 'weeping and gnashing of teeth' but of '*the* weeping and *the* gnashing of teeth' as if to emphasize the point. It is sometimes said that the problems, pressures and pains of this life make it 'a vale of tears' and it is easy to see why this is said. In the First World War, 250,000 British soldiers were killed in 100 days in the summer and autumn of 1917. Who can calculate the tears shed by their families and friends as a result of that one battle? I remember standing at the magnificent Vietnam Veterans Memorial in Washington DC, a black granite wall which at that time was inscribed with the names of 57,939 American service personnel, with an average age of eighteen, who died in that disastrous conflict. Near to where I was standing a man knelt quietly in front of one of the names. As tears welled up in his eyes I wondered how many other tears had been shed over Vietnam in the previous thirty years, and how many more as a result of all the other wars in human history.

What of all the tears shed in concentration camps and torture chambers, or those caused by accident or injury, sickness and disease, violence and bloodshed? What of the tears caused by rumour and gossip, lies and libel, poverty and neglect, tension and depression? It is impossible to imagine all the agony involved, yet even if we could find a way of quantifying it, we would still fall infinitely short of hell's weeping and the gnashing of teeth. It has been said that the weeping in hell will be such that 'the gripings and grindings of all the diseases and torments that men can or do suffer in this life are like flea bites to it.'

FIRE

By far the Bible's most frequent picture of hell is that of *fire*, and it is the one most people—even those who doubt or deny that hell exists—think of whenever hell is mentioned. There is not space in a booklet of this size to do more than mention a few of the Bible's references to hell as fire, but they will be enough to underline the fact. The last chapter in the Old Testament warns us, 'The day is coming, burning like an oven, when all the arrogant and all evildoers will be stubble. The day that is coming shall set them ablaze, says the LORD of hosts, so that it will leave them neither root nor branch.'[34] In his teaching about the day of final judgement, Jesus spoke of those who will be told, 'Depart from me, you cursed, into the eternal fire prepared for the devil and his angels.'[35] Elsewhere in the New Testament we are told of those who face 'a fearful expectation of judgement, and a fury of fire.'[36] In the last book of the Bible we read of those who will be 'thrown into the lake of fire.'[37]

In trying to understand what this means we must begin by realizing that the fire of hell is symbolic, not material. It could not drive a steam engine, generate electricity, or burn anything down. In the same way, when Jesus spoke of a 'worm' in hell, he was using a symbol, not referring to a gigantic, man-eating grub.

---

[34]   Malachi 4:1

[35]   Matthew 25:41

[36]   Hebrews 10:27

[37]   Revelation 20:15

Again, when the Bible refers to 'the wine of God's wrath'[38] we are not to think of it as being an alcoholic drink. Fire is a metaphor for hell, but as it is the one the Bible uses more than any other it is hugely important that we know what it means. What the Bible calls 'fire' is the greatest factor that makes hell to be hell, and this is nothing less than *the presence of God!*

Even for many of those who believe that hell is a terrible reality, the idea that God will be there comes not just as a shock but as something they refuse to believe. They picture God as living exclusively in heaven, eternally removed from the horrors of hell, and being loving and kind to everyone. But in thinking like this they are overlooking at least three things the Bible says.

The first is that God is *everywhere*, and as he is 'spirit'[39] is neither localized nor limited. He is not bound by time, space or the vastness of the universe, but is everywhere at all times, though not necessarily in the same way or for the same purpose. One Old Testament writer asked him, 'Where shall I go from your Spirit? Or where shall I flee from your presence? If I ascend to heaven, you are there! If I make my bed in Sheol, you are there!'[40] As we saw earlier, the word *Sheol* is sometimes used as a name for hell, and this is obviously the case here, where it is contrasted to heaven.

The second tightens things even further, as both the Old and New Testaments describe God as 'a consuming

---

[38]   Revelation 14:10

[39]   John 4:24

[40]   Psalm 139:7-8

fire.'[41] There are several times in Old Testament history at which in his righteous anger God intervened to destroy his people's enemies by fire because of their vile and vicious behaviour. In the New Testament this picture is carried forward to the final judgement, when we are told that God's enemies will be consumed by 'a fury of fire.'[42]

The third makes the presence of God in hell even clearer. Writing about the disaster that would overcome a pagan king of that time, an Old Testament prophet stated, 'A burning place has long been prepared... its pyre made deep and wide, with fire and wood in abundance; the breath of the LORD, like a stream of sulphur, kindles it.'[43] Many prophecies like this refer not only to events that were soon to happen, but also to events at the end of time, and this is a case in point. In the Bible's final book we are told that the ungodly 'will be tormented with fire and sulphur in the presence of the holy angels and *in the presence of the Lamb*.'[44] Over thirty times in that book the title 'the Lamb' is given to the Lord Jesus Christ, the eternal Son of God, so it is clear that hell's fire is not something he causes by remote control. It does not happen in God's absence, but by the 'breath' of his holy, sin-hating presence.

People sometimes think of hell as being eternal separation from God, but the Bible never uses that term.

---

[41]   Deuteronomy 4:24; Hebrews 12:29

[42]   Hebrews 10:27

[43]   Isaiah 30:33

[44]   Revelation 14:10

Instead, it warns the ungodly of the appalling experience they will have of spending eternity in God's *presence*. The French philosopher Jean-Paul Sartre, who was brought up in church circles but later 'stopped associating' with God and became a passionate atheist, said, 'The last thing I want is to be subject to the unremitting gaze of a holy God.' Yet this will be the appalling fate of all who are in hell. They will be exposed to the awesome fire of God's righteous presence, without even a glimmer of the love, mercy, kindness and compassion God offered to them while they lived on earth. This means that trying to run away from God is the most futile thing anyone can ever do. Every moment we live takes us closer to the moment when we will stand in his presence for ever, either in heaven or in hell.

HELL IS FAIR

As we saw earlier, we all have a built-in sense of justice, even though we are sometimes tempted to ignore it when it suits us to do so. Yet too often what we find in life is not only that justice is not seen to be done, but that it is often not done at all. Some people get away with murder (literally and otherwise), the innocent suffer, cheats prosper and crime pays: not always, but often enough to make it seem that justice in life struggles to stay on its feet. The only satisfying answer to the injustices of this world would be perfect justice in the world to come, but for millions of people what has been said in this booklet so far raises a massive question: *How can it be just for a God of love to send anyone to hell?*

The question is understandable, but it is the wrong question, or at least it has to be seen alongside another one: *How can an utterly holy God let any sin into heaven?* In this chapter we will look at both.

THE FIRST QUESTION

One theologian who wrestled with this question, then decided there was no answer to it, wrote, 'Everlasting torment is intolerable from a moral point of view because it makes God into a bloodthirsty monster who maintains an everlasting Auschwitz for victims whom he does not even allow to die.' He was saying that sending someone to hell is not a loving thing to do, and that if God is a God of love he could never do it. Countless people take the same line, and feel that the question has been answered, or at least side-stepped. But has it?

The Bible speaks of God's love hundreds of times, and in doing so uses some of the most beautiful language in literature. God's love is not a fluctuating emotion that comes and goes, or has highs and lows; it is part of his unchanging nature. One of the greatest statements in the Bible crams this truth into just three words: 'God is love.'[45] This is not the same as saying, 'love is God.' Nor is love merely something God has; it is an integral part of his very essence. It is not a sloppy sentimentalism that lets us get away with anything we choose to do, then when we die brushes all our failures aside and treats us as if they had never happened.

Yet there is much more to God than love, and it is dangerous to argue against the likelihood of anyone going to hell by singling out one of God's attributes and assuming that in deciding people's eternal destinies this is the only one that comes into play. As an article in

---

[45]   1 John 4:8

Punch put it, 'You can't just have the bits of God you like and leave out the stuff you're not happy with.'

It is even wrong to say that love is God's dominant characteristic. The attribute of God that stands out more than any other in Scripture is not his love but his holiness. In the Bible, his name is called his 'holy name' more often than all other descriptions taken together. In one place, the word is used three times in a single sentence. This is when the prophet Isaiah sees a vision of heaven in which angelic beings cry out, 'Holy, holy, holy is the LORD of hosts; the whole earth is full of his glory!'[46] In his perfect holiness, God is utterly intolerant of sin. Anything that falls short of his own perfection is an abomination to him, and we dare not ignore this.

God is both loving and holy, has zero tolerance of sin, and can never act in a way that contradicts his character. Those who imagine that because God is love they can live as they please, then rely on his love to keep them out of hell are making a fatal mistake.

Asking how a God of love can send people to hell misses an important point, because 'people' is a neutral word, and can give the impression that God simply decides to send some people to hell, but not others. But God does not send 'people' to hell; he sends *sinners* to hell. This does not mean we can say 'God is hate' or 'God is anger,' but it does mean that in condemning sinners he is expressing his holy hatred of sin and executing his perfectly fair and righteous judgement.

---

[46]   Isaiah 6:3

Many reading this may think they will not be condemned in this way, as they do not consider themselves to be sinners. They would hardly claim to be perfect, but they live decent, socially respectable lives, and may even believe in God and at times try to live as they think he would like them to. As this is such a crucially important issue, we need to be clear about how the Bible defines sin and who it identifies as sinners. Two statements will give us the answers.

When a deeply religious man asked Jesus which was the greatest of God's commandments, he was told, 'You shall love the Lord your God with all your heart and with all your soul and with all your mind. This is the great and first commandment.'[47] Respectability comes a long way short of this, and so does any kind of religious activity, however sincere it might be. I have never met anyone who claims to have kept what Jesus called 'the great and first commandment' and as any failure to keep it can be called the greatest and first sin, none of us can avoid the obvious implication.

The second is the straightforward statement that 'all have sinned and fall short of the glory of God.'[48] The phrase 'all have sinned' is in the past tense and tells us that none of us has a perfect track record. We may not have sinned in the same way, or to the same degree, or with the same knowledge of what we were doing, but we have all sinned, and one sin is enough to make us guilty before God and deserving of his judgement. The

[47]   Matthew 22:37-38

[48]   Romans 3:23

phrase 'and come short of the glory of God' is in the present tense and tells us that even at our best we are failing to reflect in our lives the glory of our Creator. We all know perfectly well that we fall short of our own standards, however low we set the bar. As that is the case, we should not find it difficult to confess that we fall even further short of God's standards, and are therefore sinners in his sight.

What is more, when God condemns sinners to hell he is responding to choices *they* made while they were alive. There is no law that compels people to lie, steal or cheat, or to be proud, envious, selfish, jealous or immoral. Nor is anyone forced to live a self-centred life, ignoring God and rejecting his claims. Nobody is prevented from worshipping God, thanking him for his loving kindness, and trying to live in a way that is pleasing to him. Yet countless people have little or no time for God, and generally act as if he did not exist. As Jesus put it, 'The light has come into the world, and people loved the darkness rather than the light.'[49] In other words, they not only fall short of God's standards, they deliberately ignore them and go through life making their own moral choices without realizing that these have eternal consequences. This is why C. S. Lewis wrote that at the end of the day there are only two kinds of people—those who will say to God, 'Your will be done' and those to whom God will say, 'Your will be done.' The second group will be in hell as a direct result of their own choices. Writing of how we treat God in time and how God will treat us in eternity, the Bible

---

[49]   John 3:19

says, 'If we deny him, he also will deny us.'[50] Why is that not fair?

THE SECOND QUESTION

The Bible tells us a great deal about heaven, and refers to it over 500 times, yet its glorious perfection is not only beyond our imagination, but also beyond our vocabulary. This is why in his excellent book *Grace—Amazing Grace,* Brian Edwards introduces the subject of heaven by saying, 'We are about to describe the indescribable, explain the inexplicable and keep a steady eye on the invisible.' Bible descriptions of heaven are almost all in the form of symbols, metaphors and images that take us further than plain language ever could, yet there are times when it gives us glimpses of what it is like by telling us of things that will *not* be there. To give just one example, we are told, 'Death shall be no more, neither shall there be mourning, nor crying nor pain.'[51] That one statement takes heaven far beyond our understanding, as death, mourning, crying and pain are all part and parcel of life here on earth, and it is impossible to imagine their total absence.

A head teacher friend of mine has a theory that in this life we use only two per cent of our brain capacity, but in heaven we will need the other ninety-eight per cent to take in its wonder! Be that as it may, the Bible teems with positive things about heaven and says that in

---

[50]   2 Timothy 2:12

[51]   Revelation 21:4

the future there will be 'a new heaven and a new earth.'[52] A college I once visited has the motto, 'Beyond the best there is a better' and it reminds me that heaven is infinitely better than the very best experiences we have in this life. Every pure longing we have for love, joy, peace, beauty, goodness and pleasure will be completely and eternally fulfilled. This is because those who are there will revel in experiencing for ever the very purpose for which they were created. They will know the presence of all good and the absence of all evil. As Brian Edwards puts it, 'Heaven is a new everything of which there can be nothing better.'

Yet the greatest thing of all about heaven—greater than the absence of all pain, sorrow, suffering and sin, and greater even than the fulfillment of every personal longing we have in this life—is that it is first and foremost *the presence of God in all his indescribable glory.* Heaven will be absolute perfection for all who are there because they will revel in God's intimate and holy presence. The Bible says they will know 'fullness of joy' and 'pleasures for evermore'[53] as they experience 'an eternal weight of glory beyond all comparison.'[54]

In this life, we all have highs and lows, good days and bad ones, excitement and boredom, success and failure, pleasure and pain and we can never be sure which will come next. There will be no such uncertainty in heaven, as God will ensure that nothing negative or harmful will

---

[52]   Revelation 21:1

[53]   Psalm 16:11

[54]   2 Corinthians 4:17

ever be there. He has determined that nothing and nobody will be allowed to pollute it or bring its perfection to an end. Those who died denying or doubting God's existence will not be there, nor will those who shut him out of their lives here on earth, set their own standards, ignored his commandments and chose to reject the love he showed them in so many ways. Those who had no desire to enjoy God's presence while they lived on earth will have no part in its enjoyment in heaven. Why is that not fair?

HELL IS FINAL

The horrors of hell are such that over the centuries people have tried to find ways of lessening its impact. One is to suggest that if God is a God of perfect justice some people's punishment will be less severe than others. After all, not all crimes committed in this life deserve the same punishment; killing your neighbour's dog is not as serious as killing your neighbour, nor is illegal parking as serious as robbing a bank. A court that handed down identical penalties for all four crimes would be guilty of perverting justice. As God is 'the righteous judge'[55] we should therefore expect his punishment of every person in hell to be justified and fair. We even harbour ideas or hopes about how some people will be punished after they have died. When the Irish politician Martin McGuinness died in 2017, much was made of his contribution to the peace process that ended the notorious thirty years of 'Troubles' in Ireland. Others looked back to the time when McGuinness was a

---

commander in the Irish Republican Army, which was responsible for thousands of deaths. The English peer Lord Tebbit had special memories of an IRA attack at The Grand Hotel, Brighton in 1984 in which his wife Margaret was left paralysed for life. When McGuinness died, Lord Tebbit said, 'I hope he will be parked in a particularly hot and unpleasant corner of hell for the rest of eternity.'

DEGREES?

Whatever we make of Tebbit's comment, Jesus often spoke about degrees of punishment in hell. To give just one example, he singled out some of the religious leaders of his day who not only enjoyed flaunting themselves in public but were also guilty of hypocrisy, pride, greed, dishonesty and extortion, including robbing widows of their resources. Jesus said that these men 'will receive the greater condemnation.'[56] There is no doubt that there will be degrees of punishment in hell, but we have only to pull some other facts together to see that this provides no comfort whatsoever.

Firstly, although not everyone in hell will suffer to the same degree, none will suffer to a small degree. The intensity of their punishment will match the gravity of their offences—and there is no such thing as a small offence. There are no 'little sins' because there is no little God to sin against. God's justice will ensure that the punishment fits the crime, but every sin committed will be treated as an offence against God's majesty and

---

[56]   Mark 12:40

authority. Nowhere in hell will provide shade from the heat of God's holy anger.

Secondly, those hoping that their religion or moral efforts will enable them to get away with a lesser degree of punishment are making the fundamental mistake of failing to realize that every day they live is adding to their punishment, not reducing it. This must be the case, because every day adds to the number of sins they have committed. People in hell would give anything to turn the clock back and commit even one sin less. This may be what Jesus meant when he said that if anyone causes Christians to sin 'it would be better for him if a great millstone were hung around his neck and he were thrown into the sea.'[57] Jesus was saying that it would have been better for them to have drowned before being able to commit that particular sin and so add to their eternal punishment. Elsewhere, the Bible says the same kind of thing when it warns the stubborn-hearted sinner who rejects God's kindness about 'storing up wrath for yourself on the day of wrath when God's righteous judgement will be revealed.'[58]

These are terrifying words. Every day sinners live, every dishonest penny they make, every unholy pleasure they enjoy, every ungrateful breath they take, is storing up God's anger against them. Their self-centred enjoyment of possessions and pastimes, food, sport, music, art, friendship and the rest will turn to ashes and increase the severity of their sentence. Even the time

---

[57]   Mark 9:42

[58]   Romans 2:5

spent arguing the case for a lighter sentence, or trying to bring it about by better behaviour, will produce exactly the opposite effect. Every moment sinners spend talking about greater or lesser degrees of punishment will guarantee that their punishment will be greater, not less.

CHANGE FOR THE BETTER?

Another idea is that those in hell may be able to improve their circumstances in order to lessen the pain, relieve the pressure, move to a better position or 'take the heat off.' When speaking at a meeting in an open-sided building on a camp in Ban Hang Nam, central Thailand, I was told that during the hot season a water sprinkler deployed on the roof could sometimes lower the temperature by two degrees Celsius; very little, but at least it provided some relief. There is not a single word in the Bible which gives any hope of hell's 'temperature' being reduced.

In this life, those serving prison sentences are sometimes paroled, given improved conditions, or granted special privileges as a reward for good behaviour. Yet there is no good behaviour in hell, because the sinner's moral compass is locked into position at the moment of death. Nobody's character changes after death; in hell, the ungodly will have no inclination to be any better than they were on earth. Nor will there be any influences, promises, incentives or encouragements to do anything that is right or good.

What is more, hell is not a place of probation but punishment, where sinners are sent not to learn a lesson but to pay a price. In our culture, imprisonment is at least partly seen as a tool of social engineering, a device to bring good out of evil. The Bible nowhere teaches that hell is meant to serve this kind of purpose. Instead, it says that hell is ordained by a just and holy God as the proper punishment for rebellion against his authority. Nowhere does it tell us that hell has any other purpose than to demonstrate the perfect justice of a holy God who has zero tolerance of sin. Whatever the intensity of the sinner's punishment in hell, it will be in accordance with the immaculate judgement of a God who knows the precise nature of every sin, all the circumstances in which it was committed, and exactly what punishment is deserved. Those condemned to spend eternity in hell will have no grounds to question the fairness of their sentence.

LOOPHOLES?

Two other loopholes have been suggested. In Chapter 1 we saw that there is no truth in the idea that we are annihilated when we die, and so will never have to face God in judgement. Yet some people imagine that there may come a point at which God will decide that no further punishment should be inflicted on those in hell, and they may then be annihilated. But why should that be the case? If the wicked are punished in hell (even if the degree of their punishment is graded to fit the extent of their sin) and are then wiped out, this would only be because God determined that they had at that point paid in full the penalty their sins deserved. But if they had endured all the punishment they deserved, surely a God of justice would then welcome them into heaven, rather than wipe them out? The idea that sinners pay their dues and are then 'rewarded' with annihilation makes no sense.

The other loophole is based on a question: 'One of the principles of justice is that the punishment should fit the crime. How can it be right for God to punish twenty, or sixty, or eighty years of sin with suffering that never ends?' This seems to be a reasonable question to ask, but it is seriously flawed. A burglary can be over in half an hour; would thirty minutes in prison be the right punishment? A person could be murdered in a few seconds; would a jail sentence of less than a minute be right? As one theologian has said, 'It is not necessarily the duration of the crime that fixes the duration of the punishment... What is decisive is the nature of the crime' and we have already seen that every sin is an assault on the sovereignty of God. As he is infinitely worthy of man's love, obedience and honour, man's obligation to give to him 'the glory due his name'[59] is infinitely great, and his failure to do so is infinitely sinful. As infinite sin demands infinite punishment, the everlasting sufferings of hell exactly fit the crime of which those concerned are guilty. They are the ultimate examples of God's perfect justice, which he alone has the right to execute.

What is more (and we touched on this earlier) the argument about the punishment needing to fit the crime ignores the issue of the sinner's continuing attitude.

---

59   Psalm 29:2

There is no such thing as repentance in hell, and as the refusal to repent is a sin deserving punishment, the punishment must and will continue indefinitely. Above all, the character of God is at stake here. God's punishment of sinners is not something done in a fit of temper which might blow over after a while. Instead, it is the outcome of his perfect justice and unchanging hatred of sin. That being the case, there will never be a time when God will 'cool off' and take a more lenient view of the sinner's stubborn rebellion. However desperately those in hell might cry to God to be annihilated and put out of their misery, God's righteous nature and their sinful nature will mean that the reply will always be 'No.'

'EVERLASTING' MEANS FOR EVER

Everything this chapter claims is based on something the Bible repeats again and again in the clearest possible way. It says that those who die without having got right with God 'will suffer the punishment of *eternal* destruction'[60] and 'a punishment of *eternal* fire.'[61] It speaks of those 'for whom the gloom of utter darkness has been reserved *for ever.*'[62] In the last book of the Bible we read of those for whom 'the smoke of their torment goes up *for ever and ever*'[63] and of a 'lake of

---

[60]   2 Thessalonians 1:9

[61]   Jude:7

[62]   Jude:13

[63]   Revelation 14:11

fire' in which God's enemies 'will be tormented day and night *for ever and ever.*'[64]

It is difficult to see how the words I have emphasized could mean anything other than the fact that hell is never-ending, and one other Bible reference will underline this. Jesus said that on the day of final judgement he will say to some, 'Depart from me, you cursed, into the eternal fire prepared for the devil and his angels' and that they would then 'go away into *eternal* punishment' while he would welcome others into '*eternal* life.'[65] 'Eternal punishment' obviously means hell, while 'eternal life' obviously means heaven, and in speaking of their duration, Jesus uses the same adjective for both. If he had wanted to say that only one destiny lasts for ever, he could hardly have chosen a worse way of doing so; if he had wanted to say that both destinies are everlasting, he could not have done so more clearly.

It is impossible to illustrate the eternal nature of hell but we can contrast it with time. The highest mountain in Great Britain is Ben Nevis, which rises just over 4,412 feet (1,345 metres) above sea level. Imagine an eagle swooping across the top of it and dislodging a single grain of soil. A hundred years later another eagle removes another grain, and a century later the same thing happens again. If this were repeated at the same rate, how many years would it take for Ben Nevis to be reduced to sea level? A computer print-out that

---

64   Revelation 20:10

65   Matthew 25: 41,46

stretched all around the equator 1,000 times would not be long enough to contain the figure—yet even that length of time is as nothing compared to the eternal duration of hell, in which there is no such thing as an hour, a day, a week, a month, a year, a century or a millennium. A character in a Tom Stoppard play asks, 'Eternity is a terrible thought. I mean, where's it going to end?' It never will.

We have now seen that hell is factual, fearful, fair, and final. This faces us with one massive and urgent question: on the basis of our own track record, our failure to live up to our own standards, let alone God's, is there any way in which we can avoid the horrors of hell and enjoy for ever the glories of heaven? The Bible asks that very question: 'How shall we escape....?'[66] As there is nothing we can do to correct our mistakes, compensate for our failures, or wipe away our sins, and as God will not be palmed off with religion, or with our own best efforts to live decent lives, our only hope would be if he himself did something amazing to rescue us.

He has...

---

[66]   Hebrews 2:3

ESCAPE!

The question, 'How shall we escape...' is one every serious-minded person should be asking, and the Bible points towards the answer by adding, '...*if* we neglect such a great salvation?' This tells us that the only way to escape the eternal punishment we deserve is to lay hold of this 'great salvation.' But what is it?

C. S. Lewis pointed towards it when he wrote, 'God has landed on this enemy-occupied territory in human form.' He did this 2,000 years ago when he came to earth in the person of Jesus Christ. In the musical *Jesus Christ Superstar*, Mary Magdalene sings, 'He's a man, he's just a man,' but this is not the case. He was certainly a man, but he was not *just* a man. He was God himself in human form. Throughout his life there was powerful evidence of this. In the first place, even though he was 'tempted as we are' he was 'without sin.'[67] He was 'without blemish or spot,'[68] the only flawless human

---

[67]   Hebrews 4:15

[68]   1 Peter 1:19

being who has ever lived on our planet. Then there were the amazing miracles he performed. He healed the blind, the deaf, the dumb, the lame, the leprous and the paralysed, and delivered 'all who were oppressed by the devil.'[69] At least three times he even brought a dead person back to life, including one man who had already been buried for four days. He could also control the natural elements. When he and his followers were caught in a fierce windstorm on the Sea of Galilee and those with him (several of them experienced fishermen) thought they were certain to be drowned, Jesus 'rebuked the wind and the raging waves, and they ceased, and there was a calm.'[70] These miracles were all signs that the claims he made for himself were true. When one of his followers told him, 'Show us the Father [i.e. God], and it is enough for us,' Jesus had no hesitation in replying, 'Whoever has seen me has seen the Father.'[71] Elsewhere, the Bible confirms this by saying that in Jesus was 'all the fullness of God.'[72]

Yet Jesus did not come into the world merely to work miracles, nor even just to claim that he was God. In the words of what we could call his own mission statement, he came 'to seek and to save the lost.'[73] He came on a rescue mission, to deliver people from the penalty their sins deserved and to secure for them an

[69]   Acts 10:38

[70]   Luke 8:24

[71]   John 14:8-9

[72]   Colossians 1:19

[73]   Luke 19:10

eternal home in heaven. As the Bible puts it, he 'came into the world to save sinners'[74] and he did so *by taking their place.* He did this in two ways.

Firstly, *in his life.* Everything he thought, said or did was perfect. He is the only person in human history of whom God could say, 'This is my beloved Son, with whom I am well pleased'[75] and Jesus had no hesitation in claiming, 'I always do the things that are pleasing to him [God].'[76] Theoretically, a person could be sure of going to heaven after death if they kept every part of God's law for every moment they lived on earth; Jesus was the only person who did that and he did so, *on behalf of others.*

Secondly, *in his death.* The Bible warns us about 'the law of sin and death,'[77] a law of cause and effect. Sin causes physical and spiritual death, and death is the result of sin; every sin carries a mandatory death sentence. Jesus had no sin, so there was no cause of death in him, yet when he was in his early thirties he allowed his enemies to kill him by crucifixion, the most horrific form of execution then known to man. The Bible calls death 'the wages of sin'[78] and in his death Jesus paid those 'wages' in full, even though there was not a trace of sin in his life. *He became as accountable for the sins of others as if he had been responsible for them.* The

---

[74]   1 Timothy 1:15

[75]   Matthew 17:5

[76]   John 8:29

[77]   Romans 8:2

[78]   Romans 6:23

53

complete punishment for every sin of every person in whose place he died was borne by him in his body and spirit when he died on the cross. In the death of Jesus, God's holiness, his hatred of sin and his perfect justice came together and took the life of the only sinless person in human history. When one of the best-known Christian creeds says that in his death Jesus 'descended into hell' it is not exaggerating. He did not go 'down' anywhere physically, but he bore in full hell's punishment for those in whose place he died.

There has never been a greater demonstration of love in human history. As one New Testament writer puts it, 'By this we know love, that he laid down his life for us.'[79] Jesus allowed himself to suffer the full impact of God's holy anger to enable others, who deserved to experience it, to get right with God and so avoid eternal punishment. As the Bible explains, 'Christ... suffered once for sins, the righteous for the unrighteous, *that he might bring us to God.*'[80] Within three days there was powerful proof that his death had achieved its purpose, as he 'was declared to be the Son of God in power... *by his resurrection from the dead.*'[81] In the death of Jesus all the demands of God's holy law had been met, his perfect justice had been satisfied, and his awesome anger against those in whose place Jesus died had been vented in full. His resurrection proved that he was victorious over sin, death and hell.

---

[79]   1 John 3:16

[80]   1 Peter 3:18

[81]   Romans 1:4

This is the 'great salvation' that, in his amazing love, God offers: 'For God so loved the world, that he gave his only Son, that whoever believes in him should not perish but have eternal life.'[82] To 'believe' in Jesus means more than accepting that certain facts about him are true. It means admitting that you are a sinner, having a genuine longing to turn from sin and to live in a way that is pleasing to God, then trusting in Jesus, and in him alone, to save you from the guilt and consequences of your sins. The person who refuses to do so 'is condemned already, because he has not believed in the name of the only Son of God'[83] but whoever puts their trust in him 'has eternal life. He does not come into judgement, but has passed from death to life.'[84] Eternal life is not something that begins after death. It begins the moment a person puts their trust in 'our great God and Saviour Jesus Christ.'[85]

If you have never done this, I urge you to do so now! Left to ourselves, we are on our way to hell, but in his amazing love God has set before us the way to heaven. God promises that 'everyone who calls on the name of the Lord will be saved.'[86] What reason can you possibly have for rejecting his promise to grant forgiveness of sins and eternal life to all who do so?

---

[82]   John 3:16

[83]   John 3:18

[84]   John 5:24

[85]   Titus 2:13

[86]   Romans 10:13

APPENDIX: WHY YOU CAN TRUST THE BIBLE

The first thing to notice about the Bible is that in a unique way it claims God as its author. Although it is a collection of sixty-six books written by about forty men in two main languages, Hebrew and Greek (and just a little in another) over a period of some 1,500 years, all its writers claimed that they wrote exactly what God wanted them to write. Phrases like 'God said,' 'God spoke' and 'the word of LORD came' appear some 700 times in the first five books alone, forty times in one chapter. In the first thirty-nine books (called the Old Testament) there are nearly 4,000 direct claims to divine authorship. No other literature known to man makes such clear, consistent claims.

The same kind of thing is said in the remaining twenty-seven books (the New Testament), which sums up the claim by saying, 'All Scripture is breathed out by

God.'[87] This is claiming much more than that all the human authors were inspired; it says that all their words had been *expired* by God, who 'breathed out' exactly what they wrote down. Elsewhere, the Bible calls itself 'the living and abiding word of God.'[88] This may sound like a circular argument ('The Bible is the word of God because it says it is'), but if it is God's word, how could he point us to any higher authority to authenticate what it claims?

One reason for trusting the Bible is its remarkable accuracy in recording historical facts which modern archaeology and other research are constantly confirming. To give just one example, its details of the names and reigns of about forty kings living over a period of 1,600 years are so accurate that one of the world's most brilliant scholars in the field claimed that the chance of this being a coincidence is one in 750,000,000,000,000,000,000,000,000.

Another is its amazing unity. Its forty human authors included a king, a statesman, a civil servant, a doctor, at least two fishermen, and a tent-maker. They lived at different times and in different countries, and only a few ever met each other. They probably had as many different opinions on current affairs as we would hear today on a chat show or on social media. Yet without any collaboration, spin-doctoring or technology their central message has an astonishing unity. One scholar has said that it is like the conductor of an orchestra

---

[87]   2 Timothy 3:16

[88]   1 Peter 1:23

pulling all the instruments together to produce one harmonious piece of music.

A third reason for trusting the Bible is its amazing record in foretelling the future. About thirty per cent of it consists of prophecies. A small number have yet to be fulfilled, but none (many made hundreds of years before the event) has ever been shown to be false. The odds against this being achieved by guesswork are so massive that they are not worth considering—but if God told the prophets what to write we should expect they would get it right every time; they did.

In the fourth place, there is the unique power of the Bible's message in transforming not only individual lives but entire societies for the better. Over the centuries, countless millions testify that the Bible's message has revolutionized the moral quality of their lives, making them better husbands, wives, parents, children, employers, employees, neighbours, in fact better *human beings*. It has been calculated that seventy-five percent of the social revolution that swept Western society in the eighteenth and nineteenth centuries was driven by biblical teaching, with William Wilberforce (the abolition of slavery), Elizabeth Fry (prison reform), the Seventh Earl of Shaftesbury (caring for the mentally ill) and Thomas Barnardo (housing destitute children) among those taking leading parts. Today, almost all countries where freedom, justice and tolerance are the norm have been influenced at some time by the Bible's teaching.